Franklin Watts
First published in Great Britain in 2017 by The Watts Publishing Group

Credits
Series Editor: John C. Miles
Series Designer: Richard Jewitt
Picture researcher: Diana Morris
Picture Credits: Ancient Art & Archaeology Collection: 19c. Anteromite/Shutterstock: 2-3 bg, 30-31 bg, 32 bg. Mauricio Anton/SPL: 5t. Esteban de Armas/Shutterstock: 13tr. Nick Ashton, Simon G. Lewis, Isabelle De Groote, Sarah M. Duffy, Martin Bates, Richard Bates, Peter Hoare, Mark Lewis, Simon A. Parfitt, Sylvia Peglar, Craig Williams, Chris Stringer/CC Wikimedia Commons: 4-5. Andrew Astbury/Shutterstock: 25br. Jule Berlin/Shutterstock: 22-23, 23tr. Trustees of the British Museum, London: 13c, 15c. Celtic Collection/Homer Sykes/Alamy: front cover main, 24-25. Clearview/Alamy: 15tr. Cranach/Shutterstock: front cover t, 1t. Judith Dobie/Historic England Archive: 19tr. Werner Forman Archive: 27c. Filip Fuxa/Shutterstock: 1c, 28-29. Michael Greenhaigh/CCWikimedia Commons: 21c. Anan Kaewhammui/Shutterstock: 28r. Thomas Lenne/Shutterstock: back cover tl. LuFeeTheBear/Shutterstock: front cover bg, 1 bg. Sandy Maya Matzen/Shutterstock: 11tr. Natural History Museum, London/Alamy: 7c, 9tr. Natural History Museum, London/SPL: 11c. Michael Pitts/Nature PL/Alamy: 16-17. Stewart Smith/Shutterstock: 20-21. St Nick/Shutterstock: 7tr. Jeff Tucker/Alamy: 8-9. udra11/Shutterstock: front cover bg c, 1 bg c. Nicolette Wollentin/Shutterstock: 17tr. World History Archive/Alamy: 27tr. Bjoern Wylezich/Shutterstock: back cover br.

HB ISBN 978 1 4451 5210 3
PB ISBN 978 1 4451 5211 0

Printed in China

MIX
Paper from responsible sources
FSC® C104740
www.fsc.org

Franklin Watts
An imprint of
Hachette Children's Group
Part of The Watts Publishing Group
Carmelite House
50 Victoria Embankment
London EC4Y 0DZ

An Hachette UK Company
www.hachette.co.uk

www.franklinwatts.co.uk

CONTENTS

The first people
THE HAPPISBURGH FOOTPRINTS

The Stone Age is the time when the first humans lived on Earth. They used stone tools and did not yet know how to make metal. The earliest humans of all lived in the oldest part of the Stone Age, called the Palaeolithic (pay-leo-lithic), from around 2.8 million years ago to 10,000 years ago. In Britain the earliest signs of human life are footprints made 850,000 years ago.

Around **850,000** BCE
PALAEOLITHIC

DATE FOUND: THE FOOTPRINTS WERE SPOTTED IN 2013 BY AN EXPERT IN PALAEOLITHIC TIMES.

PLACE FOUND: HAPPISBURGH BEACH, NORFOLK.

In 2000 a man walking his dog on Happisburgh Beach found a hand axe, a tool used by Stone Age humans to cut up meat. Archaeologists took a closer look at the site and found lots of other stone tools. It was the earliest evidence of people in Britain. In 2013 one of the experts spotted a set of footprints in a layer of sediment (mud) that had been uncovered on the beach by a stormy sea. They turned out to be the oldest footprints ever found outside Africa.

Archaeologists only had a couple of weeks to study the footprints (shown below) before they were washed away. They took 3-D scans of the prints and samples of the mud around them. They were able to date the mud to 850,000 years ago.

The early humans who left the footprints did not look exactly like us. They were from an early branch of the human family called Homo antecessor *and probably looked more like chimps walking upright.*

Early humans were hunter-gatherers. They hunted wild animals for food and gathered wild plants to eat. They didn't live in one place. Instead they travelled around looking for creatures to hunt.

We can tell from the footprint shapes that there were men, women and children in the group who made the footprints at Happisburgh. They were probably on a journey to find food.

Early humans made their tools by flint-knapping – using a round stone like a hammer to knock flakes off a lump of flint. The tools they made were teardrop shaped, with sharp edges, to cut meat or wood.

Have you ever made footprints in mud? Perhaps archaeologists will find them in the future!

Extra-special skull
SWANSCOMBE WOMAN

The earliest human remains so far found in Britain came from West Sussex. The find was a piece of leg bone belonging to a man who lived half a million years ago. A skull found in Kent turned out to be the earliest woman so far discovered. She lived around 400,000 years ago. Experts studying bones from these early times have found that our early ancestors had a different face and body shape to modern humans.

Around
850,000 BCE
PALAEOLITHIC

DATE FOUND:
1935, STICKING OUT OF A CLIFF FACE IN A QUARRY.

PLACE FOUND:
SWANSCOMBE, KENT.

Dentist Alvan Marston's hobby was looking for Stone Age tools. One day he was searching in a quarry in Swanscombe, Kent, when he noticed a piece of bone. It turned out to be part of a very special skull – part of the head of Swanscombe Woman. Eventually three pieces were found – the sides and the back of the skull. They fitted together like the pieces of a jigsaw.

We can tell the skull was female because of the thickness and shape of the bones. Male skulls have thicker bones and a slightly different shape at the back.

Swanscombe Woman may be an early ancestor of the Neanderthals, a branch of the human family tree who lived in Europe at this time. They were short and muscular, with low jutting brows, big noses and no chin.

Inside the skull there are faint impressions of blood vessels and folds in the woman's brain. We can tell it was similar in size to modern brains.

We know from animal bones found at Swanscombe that elephants, hyenas, rhinos and cave lions lived in the area in Palaeolithic times. The cave lions were about 10 per cent bigger than the modern lion shown above!

Lots of flint tools have been found in Swanscombe, so it looks as if early humans often visited. But they wouldn't have stayed all year round. They would have moved from place to place, looking for food.

Do you think you would be good at searching for all your food in the countryside?

Modern man + magic
GOAT'S HOLE CAVE

The first modern-looking humans, called *Homo sapiens*, began to spread out from Africa around 60,000 years ago. The earliest modern human so far found in Britain died around 33,000 years ago and was carefully buried in a cave in Wales. His companions prepared the burial in a special way, the first evidence in Britain of people believing something about life after death and perhaps having a burial ceremony of some kind.

Around **31,000** BCE

PALAEOLITHIC

DATE FOUND:
1823, IN A SEA CAVE AT THE BOTTOM OF A STEEP CLIFF.

PLACE FOUND:
GOAT'S HOLE CAVE, PAVILAND, WALES.

In Victorian times, the Reverend William Buckland heard about a Welsh sea cave full of ancient animal bones. He decided to explore, and he soon found human remains. He did not have the scientific know-how that archaeologists have today, and because the remains of a Roman fort were nearby he mistook the bones for a Roman woman, calling her the 'Red Lady'. We now know the bones belonged to a young man from Paleolithic times.

The man died around the age of 21 but we don't know how he died. He probably travelled around with a group of people looking for animals to hunt.

The man's body was covered in a red powder called ochre, and as the body rotted away the ochre coloured the bones red. His grave was marked with a mammoth skull. Perhaps his companions believed these things had magical powers.

At the time of the burial the cave would have been many miles from the sea, overlooking a plain. Britain's landscape has changed greatly since the man died.

The young man was buried with mysterious rods made of ivory. They might have been used in some sort of ceremony, but it's impossible to know for sure.

Have you been to a ceremony (such as a wedding or a funeral) where special objects were used in some way?

Butchered bones
GOUGH'S CAVE

A collection of bones from different people have been found in Gough's Cave in Somerset. The fragments date to different times in the Stone Age. The finds include the oldest complete skeleton ever found in Britain, bones that were butchered and eaten by canaibals, and skulls that were made into cups!

Between
12,700 BCE
- 7,000 BCE
LATE
PALAEOLITHIC

DATE FOUND:
FINDS HAVE BEEN
TURNING UP IN THE
CAVE SINCE 1903.

PLACE FOUND:
CHEDDAR,
SOMERSET.

Gough's Cave was opened as a tourist attraction at the beginning of the 1900s. When it was being cleared out the first ancient bones were found, and more were discovered in the 1980s. Archaeologists have recently used the latest scientific techniques on the finds and made new discoveries about them. Powerful microscopes have shown up tell-tale marks made by cannibals on some of the bones. The cannibals were in the cave around 14,700 years ago.

Some of the human bones found in the cave had cut marks on them made by flint tools used to cut off meat. Chew marks on some of the bones proved that they had been gnawed.

Three of the skulls that were found in the cave had been made into cups. Shortly after people died the skulls were cleaned out and shaped. One of the cups is shown below.

The cave system at Cheddar is extensive. Other Stone Age remains have been found there, including the earliest complete human skeleton found in Britain, dating to 10,000 years ago.

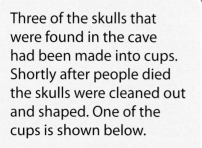

Lots of animal bones were found along with the butchered human bones, so we know that the cave campers weren't forced to be cannibals because they were hungry. Perhaps they ate their dead relatives or enemies in some sort of ceremony.

Can you imagine camping in a dark cave like Gough's Cave?

Ice Age artists
CRESWELL CAVES

During Palaeolithic times there were intensely cold eras we call Ice Ages, when Britain was covered in thick ice like the Antarctic is today, and it was too cold for anyone to survive. In between the Ice Ages the climate warmed up and people ventured back to Britain from further south to hunt for food and animal skins. Bands of these hunters sheltered in Creswell Caves in Nottinghamshire and left behind the first art found in Britain.

Around **10,000** BCE LATE PALAEOLITHIC

DATE FOUND: THE HORSE BONE WAS FOUND IN 1876. LOTS MORE REMAINS HAVE BEEN FOUND AROUND THE CAVES SINCE.

PLACE FOUND: CRESWELL CAVES, NOTTINGHAMSHIRE.

In Victorian times people began to find ancient remains in Creswell Caves, and archaeologists have been studying them ever since. The finds prove that Stone Age hunters came here over thousands of years, using the caves to shelter on their hunting trips. They left behind lots of flint tools and even a sewing needle made from bone. Around 12,500 years ago someone left behind an animal bone with a beautiful carving of a horse on it.

Some of the cave visitors were skilled artists, good at creating a shape that everyone could recognise. The horse carving is on a piece of animal rib, and shows the front part of a horse. It has lines across it that could perhaps represent spears.

At the time the horse picture was made, the last Ice Age was coming to an end in Britain. It would still have been an icy cold place, though. Hunters would have had to wrap up warmly in animal furs.

The bone has been made shiny by someone touching it many times. Perhaps they touched it to bring them good luck before they went hunting, though we can only guess at that.

We know that the hunters who camped at Creswell killed and ate lots of hare meat, because they left the animal bones behind. They would have used the skin and fur to make clothes.

Can you imagine camping in a wintry land, wearing animal skins for clothes?

A long-lost lake
STAR CARR

The middle part of the Stone Age, between 10,000 BCE and 4,000 BCE, is called the Mesolithic (mee-zoh-lithic). It is the name given to the period between the end of the last Ice Age and the time when people began farming. Some Mesolithic people set up camp by a lake at Star Carr in Yorkshire, where they left behind some mysterious headdresses and the remains of Britain's first home.

Around
9,000 BCE
MESOLITHIC

DATE FOUND:
THE FIRST DISCOVERIES WERE MADE IN 1949, BUT NEW SURPRISES ARE STILL TURNING UP ON THE SITE!

PLACE FOUND:
STAR CARR, YORKSHIRE.

In 1949 a local man was walking across a field when he saw a flint tool sticking up. It was the first find on this important site. Soon archaeologists discovered lots more tools made from stone and animal bones, along with 21 antler headdresses. There was a lake at Star Carr 11,000 years ago, and the waterlogged soil around the lake helped to preserve the objects.

The deer antler headdresses had holes made in them, probably for leather strings. Using the strings, someone could tie a headdress on to their head like a hat.

People might have worn the headdresses for a ritual dance, to make sure they had a good hunt. They might even have worn them during the hunt itself, as a disguise to sneak up on deer.

Archaeologists found a ring of post holes – holes that once held timber posts. The holes are evidence of the earliest home so far found in Britain. The posts would have stretched up to make a teepee shape.

This is a reconstruction of an early teepee-shaped home, probably similar to the home at Star Carr. It may have had reed thatch and timbers tied together with string made from nettle fibre or wild honeysuckle.

Can you imagine living in a teepee-shaped home like the one at Star Carr?

Underwater treasure
BOULDNOR CLIFF

Around 8,000 years ago a huge landslide in Norway caused a tsunami – a giant 10-m-high wave – which flooded thousands of kilometres of land between Britain and Europe and made Britain into an island. Diving archaeologists have found some surprises preserved from those times, hidden under the seabed off the Isle of Wight.

Around
6,500 BCE
LATE MESOLITHIC

DATE FOUND:
THE FIRST DISCOVERIES WERE MADE IN THE 1970S. FINDS ARE STILL BEING DISCOVERED AND ANALYSED.

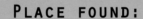

PLACE FOUND:
IN THE SEA NEAR BOULDNOR ON THE ISLE OF WIGHT.

In the 1970s fishermen trawling near a cliff off the coast of the Isle of Wight were puzzled to find bits of timber in their nets. The timbers turned out to be the remains of a drowned forest that grew on dry land in the time just before the big flood. Years later, diving archaeologists noticed some flint tools that had been freshly dug up by lobsters burrowing into the soft clay at the base of the cliff. The lobsters had helped to discover a Mesolithic camping site from just before the flood.

Divers found remains of the camp in mud below the seabed. They discovered that the campers here had been busy making flint tools and sharpening their axes.

The campers left behind traces of flour made from einkorn wheat (above). This is the oldest farming find in Britain, 2,000 years older than any other crop traces found in the country. We don't know if the wheat was grown nearby or brought from Europe.

Some of the timber the divers found had been deliberately cut in a certain way, possibly to make boats. If so, this would be the earliest boat-building site so far found in the whole world.

The campers had cooked and eaten freshwater fish, and left the bones of their meals behind.

Have you eaten flatbread? The campers at Bouldnor Cliff probably made a type of flatbread from their flour.

Home cooking on the farm
WINDMILL HILL POTS

Around 6,000 years ago people in Britain began to farm for the first time, growing crops and keeping animals. We call this part of the Stone Age the Neolithic (nee-oh-lithic), lasting from 4,000 BCE to 2,500 BCE. Daily life began changing for Neolithic people in many ways. For instance, they began to use clay pots to cook their food. The earliest cooking pots so far found in Britain come from Windmill Hill in Wiltshire. They would have been the latest technology when they were made!

Around
3,700 BCE
EARLY
NEOLITHIC

DATE FOUND:
1925, BY WEALTHY AMATEUR ARCHAEOLOGIST ALEXANDER KEILLER.

PLACE FOUND:
WINDMILL HILL, NEAR AVEBURY, WILTSHIRE.

When interesting finds were made at Windmill Hill in the 1920s, wealthy archaeology fan Alexander Keiller decided to buy the whole site so he could excavate it. It turned out to be one of the first Neolithic settlements ever found in Britain. It seems people were beginning to live in communities in one place instead of roaming around in separate hunting bands.

Some of the pots found at Windmill Hill came from southwest Cornwall, 185 km away. Perhaps people traded with visitors to get them, though we don't know for sure how they arrived at Windmill Hill.

The Windmill Hill pots would have been used to boil or roast food, such as meat flavoured with wild herbs and nettles. Stews and soups would have been made in Britain for the first time, using pots like this.

This artist's impression shows what Windmill Hill might have looked like. A ceremony for a dead person is going on, with everybody joining in.

Neolithic pots were often decorated with lines drawn into the wet clay. They are called grooveware because of the patterns on them. Some of the pots found at Windmill Hill were like this.

We know from bones left at the site that the Neolithic people at Windmill Hill kept cattle, pigs and goats. They had dogs to help them herd the animals.

Have you ever made a clay pot? Try it to find out how difficult it is!

Top axes
LANGDALE AXE FACTORY

The axe was a very useful tool for Britain's first farmers. They could use it to cut down trees and clear land. But the axe heads that came from Cumbria were extra special. They were made high up on a dangerous mountainside, and they may even have been thought of as magical. They were prized all around Britain.

Around **3,500** BCE

NEOLITHIC

DATE FOUND:
DISCOVERED IN 1947. THEN ARCHAEOLOGISTS EXPLORED AND FOUND MORE REMAINS.

PLACE FOUND:
LANGDALE, CUMBRIA.

Pike O'Stickle and Harrison Stickle are rugged high peaks in Cumbria's Lake District. They are littered with flakes of stone called scree, and when knowledgeable mountain explorers took a look they realised that the millions of flakes were man-made rubbish from an outdoor Stone Age factory. The pieces had been knocked off lumps of stone to make shapes that could be polished and made into axe heads. Langdale turned out to be one of the first workplaces ever found in Britain.

To create a basic axe head shape, someone had to knock flakes from a block of stone. It would have taken about 45 minutes to create one axe head.

The Langdale axe makers worked very high up on dangerous ledges. They seemed to prize the stone found in the highest, most dangerous spots. Perhaps they thought that the top of the mountain was a magical place.

Nearly 30 per cent of all the Neolithic axe heads found in Britain come from Langdale. Experts can tell by looking at the stone through a microscope.

The Langdale axes were made from a type of volcanic rock called greenstone. The axe heads were taken away and polished. It would have taken many hours to polish the stone until the dark green colour shone through.

The Langdale axes might have been transported around Britain by boat. They have even been found in Ireland. They were obviously a top brand!

Langdale axes were prized possessions. Do you know where your most prized possession was made?

Trash tells a story
SKARA BRAE

Once people began to settle in one place instead of moving around all the time, they began to leave piles of rubbish outside their homes. These trash heaps are called middens. By studying the remains found in middens, we can find clues about how people lived.

Around
31,000 BCE
NEOLITHIC

DATE FOUND:
1850, AFTER A HUGE STORM EXPOSED THE REMAINS.

PLACE FOUND:
MAINLAND, THE LARGEST OF THE ORKNEY ISLANDS.

In 1850 a great storm ripped the grass off an old mound at Skara Brae, in the far north of Scotland. Underneath, archaeologists found a group of ancient homes from 5,000 years ago. People lived there for around 600 years, and left lots of rubbish behind. The food remains they threw away showed that they ate fish, cattle and sheep. They hunted red deer and boar and used animal skins to make their clothes.

The homes were built of rock with turf ceilings. Each home had a single, large, rectangular-shaped room.

Each house had a hearth for a fire. The houses would have been cosy and warm. There were stone beds. They would probably have had straw mattresses and animal skins on them.

Each house had a dresser (shelves) built against the wall, facing the door. Perhaps this was where Stone Age people kept valuable objects.

Some of the houses had stone tanks for keeping live limpets. The local people probably ate them and used them as fish bait.

The houses had no windows. They would have been dark and smoky inside.

What could people tell about your life if they looked at your rubbish?

Tribes of fur and feather
TOMB OF THE EAGLES

In late Neolithic times people began to live in tribes – communities of related people. Their bones were put inside stone burial chambers called barrows or cairns, alongside the bones of other people in their group. In the Orkney Islands there is a cairn containing some unusual bones.

Around
3,000 BCE
LATE
NEOLITHIC

DATE FOUND:
1958, BY A FARMER
IN HIS FIELD.

PLACE FOUND:
NEAR LIDDER,
ORKNEY.

When a local farmer dug up a strange stone in his Orkney field he found a Stone Age cairn, a stone passageway leading to chambers filled with human skulls. For a century or more, Neolithic people had put their dead in the cairn and held mysterious ceremonies outside, smashing burnt pots and killing calves, then leaving the meat on the ground. Alongside the human skulls there were lots of sea eagle bones and talons.

The people who used the cairn were probably a tribe who lived together on an area of territory that they claimed as theirs. Nearby tribes had their own cairns, and different ways of burying their dead.

The farmer found the polished black and white stone top of a ceremonial staff called a mace (shown far left). Perhaps it was used in burial ceremonies.

It's possible the tribe left the bodies of their dead outside in the open, to be picked clean by local sea eagles before the bones were finally put into the cairn.

It's possible the sea eagle was a totem – the magical symbol of the tribe who used the cairn. Another Orkney cairn was full of dog skulls. Perhaps the dog was the totem of the tribe who used it.

To get into a Neolithic burial chamber you must first crawl through a narrow passage. It's thought the journey might represent moving into another world – the world of the dead.

Do you have a 'tribe'? What groups of people do you belong to?

Unsolved mysteries
FOLKTON DRUMS

Many things about the Stone Age are deeply mysterious. With nothing written down from those times, we can only make our best guesses based on the clues we find. The Folkton Drums are one of the biggest British Stone Age mysteries. Why were they buried next to a child and what were they for? Check out the clues and come up with your own theory.

Around **2,500** BCE
LATE NEOLITHIC

DATE FOUND: 1889, BY A CHURCH LIBRARIAN WHOSE HOBBY WAS DIGGING UP STONE AGE BURIAL BARROWS.

PLACE FOUND: FOLKTON, NEAR FILEY IN YORKSHIRE.

There were several people buried in the barrow at Folkton, but one was special. A child had been carefully laid on a set of three drum shapes carved out of local chalk and decorated with zig-zags, swirls and eyes. We call them drums because they look drum-shaped to us, not because they were drums to play, but in truth we can't know what they were for. They are rare finds, so they were probably very valuable possessions.

There were three drums of different sizes. The biggest was 146 mm across and 107 mm high.

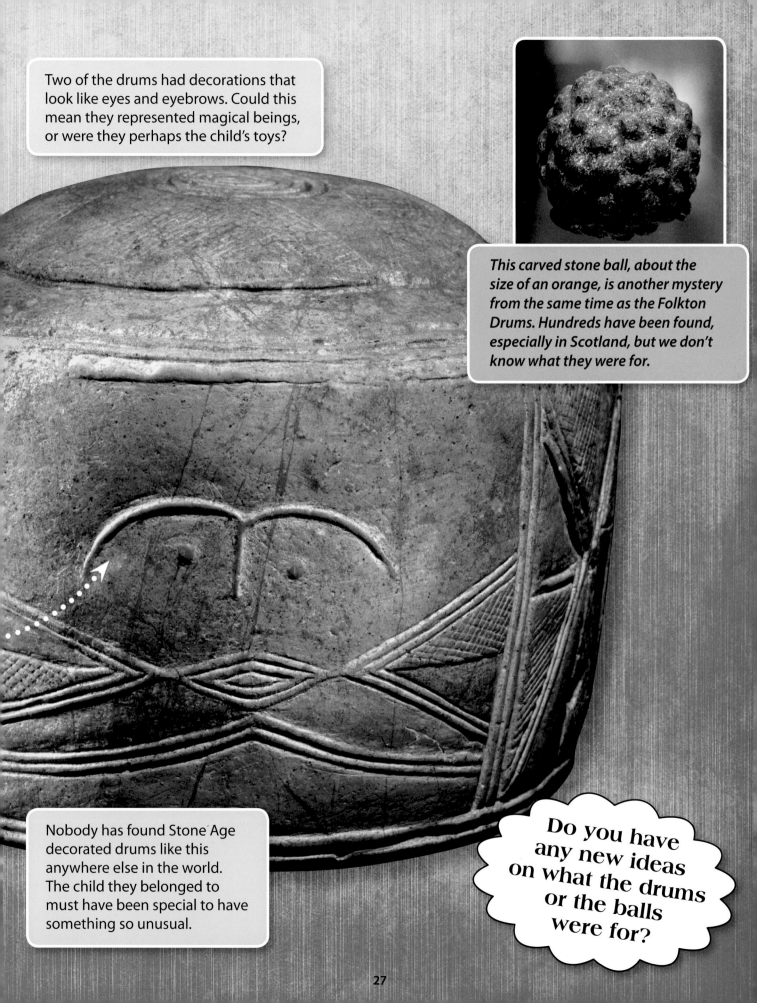

Two of the drums had decorations that look like eyes and eyebrows. Could this mean they represented magical beings, or were they perhaps the child's toys?

This carved stone ball, about the size of an orange, is another mystery from the same time as the Folkton Drums. Hundreds have been found, especially in Scotland, but we don't know what they were for.

Nobody has found Stone Age decorated drums like this anywhere else in the world. The child they belonged to must have been special to have something so unusual.

Do you have any new ideas on what the drums or the balls were for?

Sacred circle
STONEHENGE

People who lived towards the end of the Stone Age built wood and stone circles around Britain, including the most famous stone circle of all – Stonehenge in Wiltshire. They probably held religious ceremonies of some kind in these circles, and often buried their dead nearby. Archaeologists have used the latest technology around Stonehenge to discover new finds, including even more circles, and the remains of winter feasts.

DATE FOUND:
THANKS TO MODERN TECHNOLOGY NEW FINDS ARE TURNING UP ALL THE TIME AROUND STONEHENGE!

PLACE FOUND:
SALISBURY PLAIN, WILTSHIRE.

Archaeologists have been exploring the countryside around Stonehenge using ground-penetrating radar and 3-D laser scanners. They have been able to map up to 3 m underground and have discovered at least 17 smaller wooden or stone shrines nearby, as well as a Neolithic village and a giant wooden circle called Durrington Walls. We can tell that Stonehenge itself was built and rebuilt over many centuries.

Stone Age circle builders probably believed in cosmology – a magical link between the Earth and the sky. They designed Stonehenge so that the Sun's rays appeared in an exact spot between the stones at midsummer and midwinter.

There was probably a big ceremony at Stonehenge in midwinter. We know that people had midwinter feasts nearby because they left behind lots of bones from pigs that were born in spring and killed nine months later to eat.

People cremated (burnt) their dead in ceremonies near Stonehenge and sometimes buried the burnt remains in pits dug around the stones themselves.

Around 2,300 BCE the time we call the Stone Age ended and the era called the Bronze Age began – a time when people began to use bronze tools.

Stonehenge continued to be used for ceremonies at the beginning of the Bronze Age, but then it seems people's religious beliefs may have changed.

Have you been to a religious ceremony held in a special place? Did you have food at the time of the ceremony?

Glossary

archaeologist   Someone who studies bones and man-made remains from the past.

barrow   A Stone Age burial chamber built from stones and covered with a mound of earth.

cosmology   The belief in a magical link between the Earth and the sky.

cremation   The ceremonial burning of a human body.

einkorn   An early type of wheat crop.

flint-knapping   Making a tool from a lump of flint by knocking chips of flint off it to form the tool's shape.

ground-penetrating radar   A machine that sends radar pulses into the ground. They bounce back off buried objects and the resulting measurements can be used to make an underground map.

hunter-gatherer   Someone who gathers their own food by hunting animals or finding edible plants.

Ice Age   An era in the Stone Age when the climate was very cold and the land was covered in thick sheets of ice for long periods of time.

ivory   The tusks of animals, such as elephants. Ivory is made from a similar material to that which teeth are made of.

limpet   an edible sea snail with a cone-shaped shell.

mace   A ceremonial staff, usually held by an important person taking part in a ceremony.

Mesolithic   The Middle Stone Age, between 8,000 BCE and 4,000 BCE.

midden   A trash heap that contains waste items, such as bones, shells and dung.

Neanderthal   A type of early human with a shorter body than a modern human and a face with a jutting brow, big nose and no chin.

Neolithic   The New Stone Age, from 4,000 BCE to 2,500 BCE.

ochre   A type of reddish-coloured earth.

Palaeolithic   The Old Stone Age, from 2.8 million years ago to 10,000 years ago.

post hole   A hole in the ground that once held a timber post.

ritual   A series of actions performed in a certain order, usually at a ceremony.

sediment   Mud that has settled on the bottom of a riverbed or seabed.

Stone Age   A time when early humans living on Earth used stone tools. They had not yet learnt how to make metal.

totem   An animal or natural object used as a symbol, which is thought to have magical powers.

Further Information

WEBLINKS

http://www.creswell-crags.org.uk
Find out all about the hunters of Creswell Caves and play a game to see if you would survive in their world.

http://www.ancientcraft.co.uk/Archaeology/stone-age/stoneage_food.html
Try some recipes recreating Stone Age food such as hazelnut bread and nettle pudding.

http://timetravellerkids.co.uk/news/make-a-stone-age-pot/
Follow these instructions for making a Neolithic pot and a Stone Age necklace.

Note to parents and teachers: Every effort has been made by the Publishers to ensure that the websites in this book are suitable for children, that they are of the highest educational value, and that they contain no inappropriate or offensive material. However, because of the nature of the Internet, it is impossible to guarantee that the contents of these sites will not be altered. We strongly advise that Internet access is supervised by a responsible adult.

TIMELINE

2.5 million years ago   The first ape-like members of the human family appeared in Africa. The early part of the Stone Age, the Palaeolithic, dates from here. From roughly this time onwards, different branches of the human family developed, looking different to each other.

850,000 BCE   The date of the Happisburgh footprints, the oldest footprints found outside Africa. They were made by individuals in a branch of the human family called *Homo antecessor*.

500,000 BCE   The date of the earliest humanoid bone fragments found in Britain, belonging to a branch of the human family called *Homo heidelbergensis*.

98,000 BCE   A branch of the human family called Neanderthals lived in Britain.

31,000 BCE   The branch of the human family we are descended from, called *Homo sapiens* (modern humans), were living in Britain.

10,000 BCE   This date marks the beginning of the Middle Stone Age, the Mesolithic.

9,000 BCE   Mesolithic people constructed the earliest-known dwelling in Britain at Star Carr.

6,100 BCE   A giant tsunami cut Britain off from the rest of Europe.

4,500 BCE   The Late Stone Age, called the Neolithic, began. The first farmers began to grow crops in Britain.

3,000 BCE   The first ceremonial structures appeared around the area of Stonehenge.

2,500 BCE   The secret of making bronze was brought to Britain and the Bronze Age began.

Index

These are the lists of contents for titles in the FOUND! series:

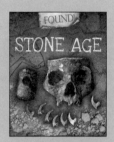

Also in the series: